Let us make this a holy place for the human spirit, consecrated to the forces which magnify the soul.

Edmund Janes James, University of Illinois president, 1904 - 1920

We aim high in hope and work, so that long after we are gone, the University of Illinois will remain a wonderful, living thing.

President Stanley O. Ikenberry

THE UNIVERSITY OF
ILLINOIS

PHOTOGRAPHED BY BARTH FALKENBERG

HARMONY HOUSE
PUBLISHERS LOUISVILLE

Foellinger Auditorium

Executive Editors: William Butler and William Strode
Library of Congress Catalog Number 87-083167
Hardcover International Standard Book Number 0-916509-19-2
Printed in USA by Pinaire Lithographing Corp., Louisville, Kentucky
First Edition printed Fall 1988 by Harmony House Publishers
P.O. Box 90, Prospect, Kentucky 40059 (502) 228-2010 / 228-4446
Copyright © 1988 by Harmony House Publishers
Photographs Copyright © 1988 by Barth Falkenberg
This book or portions thereof may not be reproduced in any form without permission of Harmony House. Photographs may noy be reproduced without permission of Barth Falkenberg.

DIANA

This photographic look at the University of Illinois in Urbana-Champaign today and yesterday is the first such book to be published in 38 years. It was in 1950 that the late Don Jackson edited *Illini Years*, a picture history published by the University of Illinois Press.

In the time since, enrollments soared. The campus experienced tremendous growth — and it continues to change, with new facilities and innovative programs that anticipate our country's needs.

The transistor and computer chip, one the brainchild of a U. of I. professor and the other of an alumnus, helped propel us toward the 21st century.

Yet the heart of the campus remains the same, both in sight and spirit. Its vitality, color, problems and pleasures are much as I remember them when I was in school more than 30 years ago. We invite you to return to share them with us. But if you can't, we believe that this book will help you to relive many happy days.

We hope that you will enjoy it and share it with your friends.

Yours for Illinois,

Louis D. Liay
Executive Director and
Chief Administrative Officer,
University of Illinois Alumni Association

English Building

On Saturday afternoon, not long ago, after a Homecoming Game, I took a walk by myself across the campus. I walked from Memorial Stadium past Krannert and then past the Library with the Lorado Taft figures eternally bent in private dreams, and then past the Auditorium and down the Quadrangle, and there was not a building I passed that did not have a memory. There in the Library I had, as a child, gone to view Audubon's birds. In front of the Auditorium I had heard John F. Kennedy speak in 1960, and inside I heard e. e. cummings read his poems. In Gregory Hall I had seen "The Maltese Falcon" for the first time, and in the English Building, read my way through Faulkner, and how many hours or days or weeks I had lingered over coffee in the Illini Union could no longer be calculated.

Looking through these photographs is like taking another walk, a slower and more thoughtful one, with even more memories. The University of Illinois is where so many of us have discovered who we were to be, and in these pages we can remember the days and places that happened.

Roger Ebert

UNIVERSITY OF ILLINOIS "FIRSTS"

1868 First architectural instruction west of the Alleghenies

1872 First architectural graduate in America, Clifford Ricker

1876 Morrow Plots, the oldest soil fertility plots in America

1877 The world's first course in general bacteriology

1881 First evidence of bacteria causing plant disease

1897 First state-supported school of music in America

1901 First university dean of men in the world

1902 First collegiate cheerleader, R.C. Matthews

1907 The birthplace of the university symphonic band

1910 First collegiate Homecoming celebration

1913 First modern sensitive photoelectric cell by Jakob Kunz

1919 First antitoxin for botulism poisoning in man

1920 First collegiate Dad's Day celebration

1921 First collegiate Mother's Day celebration

1922 First sound-on-film movies

1923 First student newspaper to have full AP wire service capabilities

1935 Discovery of the essential amino acid threonine

1939 First PhD. granted in accountancy, to J.W. McMahon

1940 Development of the first betatron for high energy physics

1948 First comprehensive college program for the severely disabled

1950 Development of world's largest betatron or "atom smasher"

1951 First scientific book published dealing with space medicine

1956 Development of a comprehensive theory of super-conductivity

1959 Development of the first computer use for direct education

1961 Development of the log-periodic antenna, as used by most television receivers

1966 First synthesis of the self-duplicating part of living matter

1970 Construction of the first visible-spectrum semi-conductor laser

1971 Invention of miniature medical operating microscope

1972 First achievement of a temperature as low as 3/1,000 of a degree above absolute zero and development of a thermometer to measure it

1977 Discovery of methanagens as a third form of life

Art and Design Building

A university is not a few classes and teachers and a place to eat and sleep, with trees and pleasant walks in between. All the wisdom of the past has been gathered here on this fertile prairie. It can supply all the answers to all your questions, except why a football bounces into the arms of the wrong man. But you have to know what is going on. A university is a vast catalogue of interesting events on the side: lectures, concerts, political, religious and dramatic societies to suit every interest and taste. You cannot digest this whole smorgasbord. You will find that every teacher thinks you have nothing to do except produce for him. But even so, you can look at the intellectual menu every morning in the Calendar of Events in the Daily Illini, *and taste the fare from time to time ... It is in these simple ways, by these practical small initiatives, that you come upon windows and doors into the wider world of the mind. Much more than my generation, most of you are going to live in the great clattering world of cities, where the enduring things of the human spirit – love and friendship and the association of lively minds – are not so easy to come by without an effort.*

For a time here in this place, a comparatively brief intermission between leaving your father's house and starting your own, you will be free to discover who you are, and where you are and what way you are going, and who's going with you.

James B. Reston of The New York Times, Convocation, September, 1965

The student who comes to the Urbana-Champaign campus finds himself in a complex, diverse community – indeed, an educational city.

Chicago Daily News, September, 1965

Previous Page: Altgeld Hall

Overleaf: Commerce Building

25

You are here, shall we agree, because you do not yet know who you are. The purpose of education is to give you this knowledge, in whatever form and to whatever extent it may be available. Perhaps it has never been fully available to any man. Perhaps? No, certainly it has never been. For a man who knew everything about himself would know everything about everything else, and there has been no such man. The limits of human knowledge are nowhere so clearly seen as here: the limits, nor the delights either, for in whatever measure we do know ourselves we are happy. And I take it that happiness is the thing we all most deeply desire..

Mark Van Doren '14

Undergraduate Library

Altgeld Hall Library

Krannert Art Museum

Krannert Center

Not every institution has a quadrangle such as that on the Urbana-Champaign campus. It is famed in song and story. If it had a voice, the Quad could tell many yarns about what it has heard and seen as the University of Illinois years have unfolded.

Chuck Flynn in the *News-Gazette*, October 19, 1986

Enough trees and shrubs were planted ... to make a noticeable difference in the bleak prairie landscape. Practically on his own responsibility Dr. Thomas J. Burrill planted the elms along the avenue which perpetuates his name, as well as many other trees which now give charm and distinction to the campus.

Leon D. Tilton in *History of the Campus of the University of Illinois*

As a student here I listened with fascination to the tales my grandfather told of that University of Illinois he had first known in the 1870's. It was hard for me to relate the tiny infant of an institution he described to the bustling university in which I labored and learned. But if in the 1930's we thought the University had become huge, just look now.

Yet the many acres of new educational buildings that surround us today are visual evidence of a special quality of our University. I don't mean its ever-burgeoning size. In these days any institution can grow large. I mean its capacity in each generation to serve the people according to the needs of that generation, in the honored land-grant tradition. The necessity and glory of any really creative institution are excellence and self-renewal. We who are its products are grateful and proud that the University of Illinois, from its earliest years, has been distinguished by fidelity to both these qualities.

Assistant Secretary of State Phillips Talbot, Commencement, 1964

42

The Morrow Plots

Within sight of the towers of the University, in the farming country to the south, stands a familiar old schoolhouse, which was built at much the same time as University Hall, and which ... expresses fairly well the crudity of public education at Illinois. To look at it is to appreciate the poverty and bareness out of which the people of Illinois had to build their educational structure, and to turn from it to the towers is to appreciate better the proportions and strength of this structure as it is now crowned in the University. In 49 years the state has raised in these corn fields an institution impressive in itself and for what it stands.

Allan Nevins in *Illinois*, 1917

Our chief institutional characteristic must continue to be comprehensiveness – comprehensiveness in service, in levels of education, in scope and nature of program. Here, I do not mean that the University can be all things to all people, but I do mean that our strength in the future, as in the past, is our role as a people's university.

Dr. David Dodds Henry, President of the University of Illinois, April, 1968

IMPE

Sorority Rush

Fraternity Rush

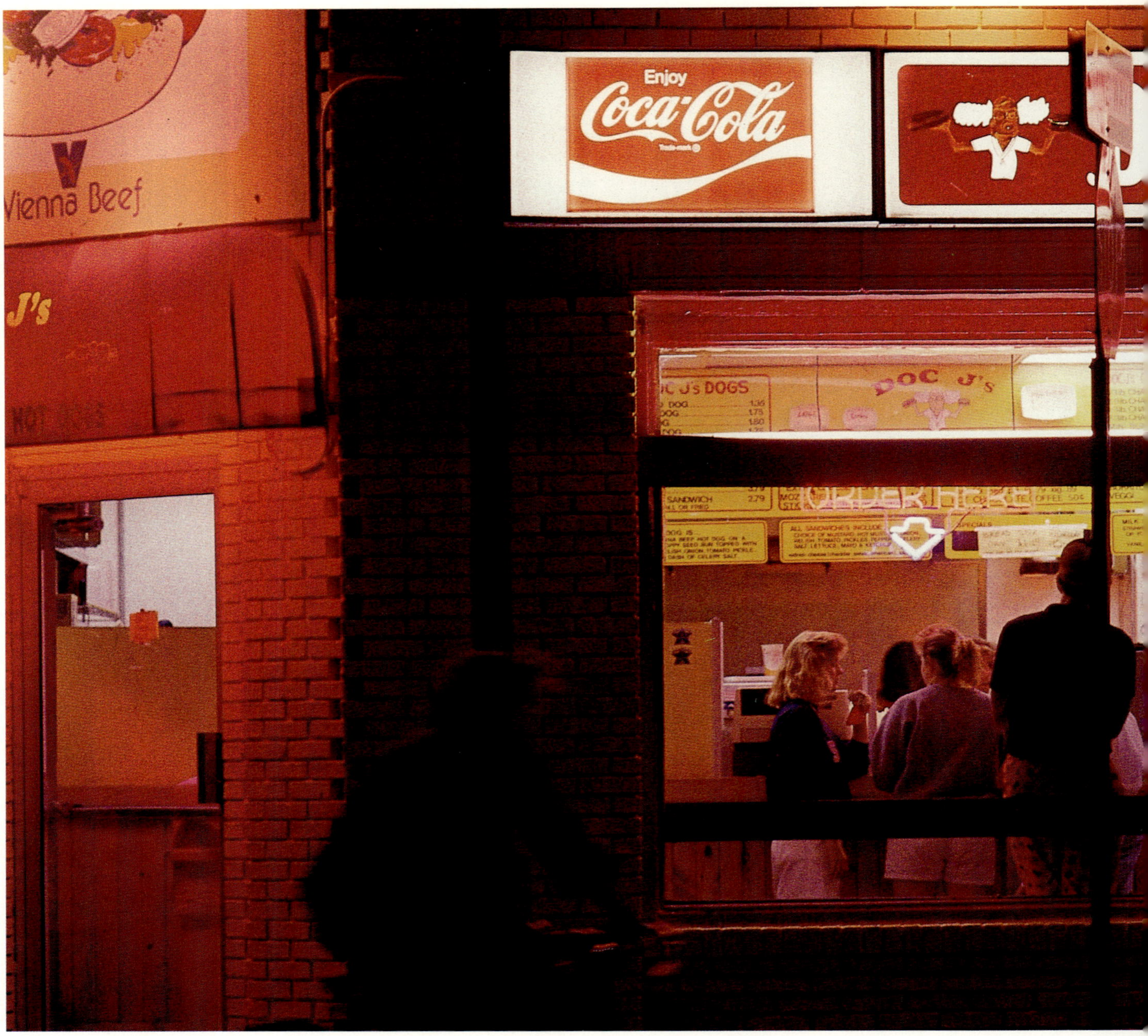
Vienna Beef
J's
Enjoy
Coca-Cola
DOC J's
ORDER HERE

ILLINI INN
SERVING ILLINI SINCE 1935
BUSCH
Stroh's
Budweiser
BUD LIGHT

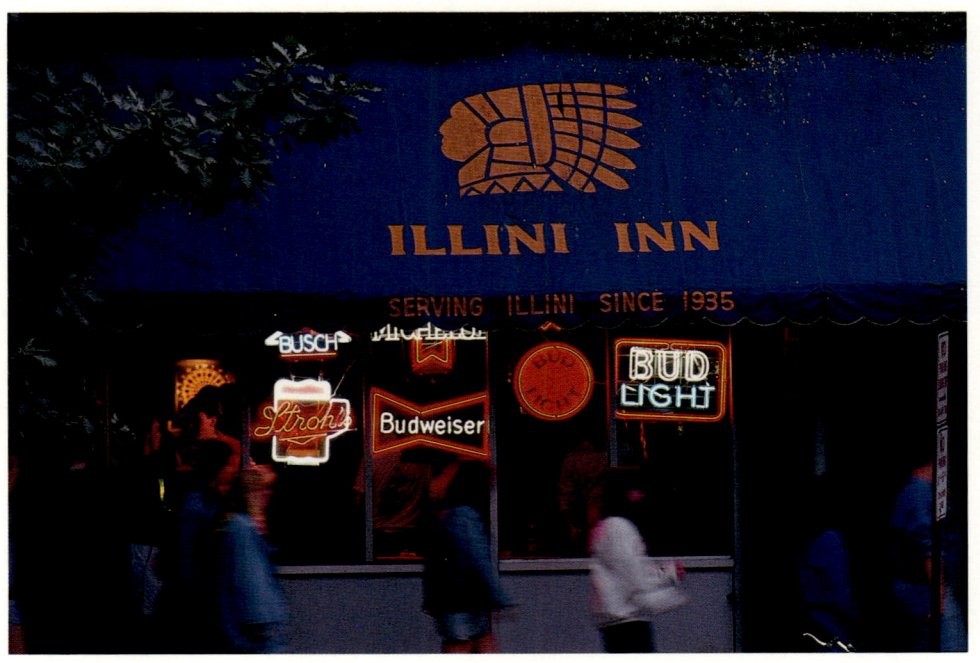

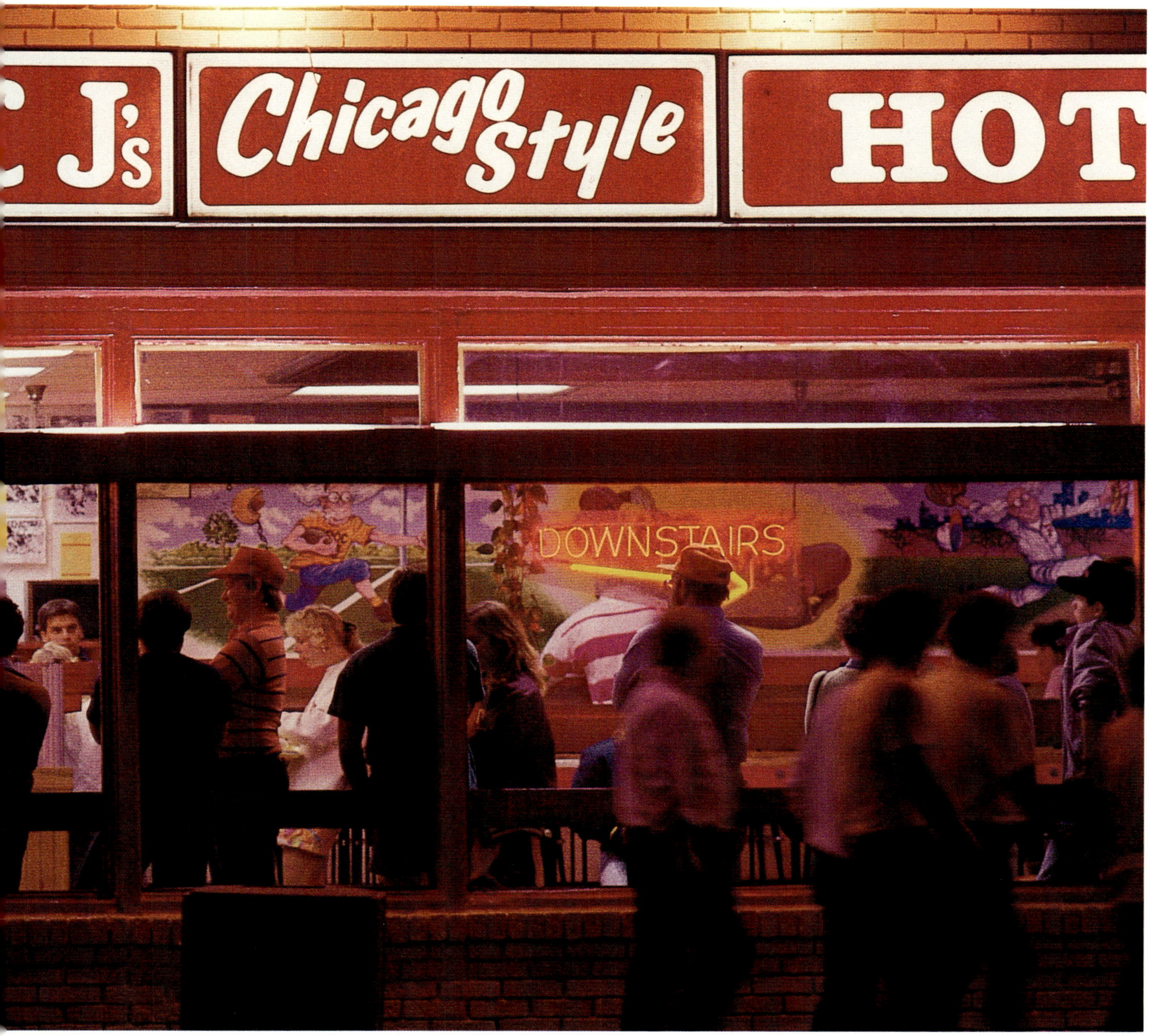
C J's
Chicago Style
HOT
DOWNSTAIRS

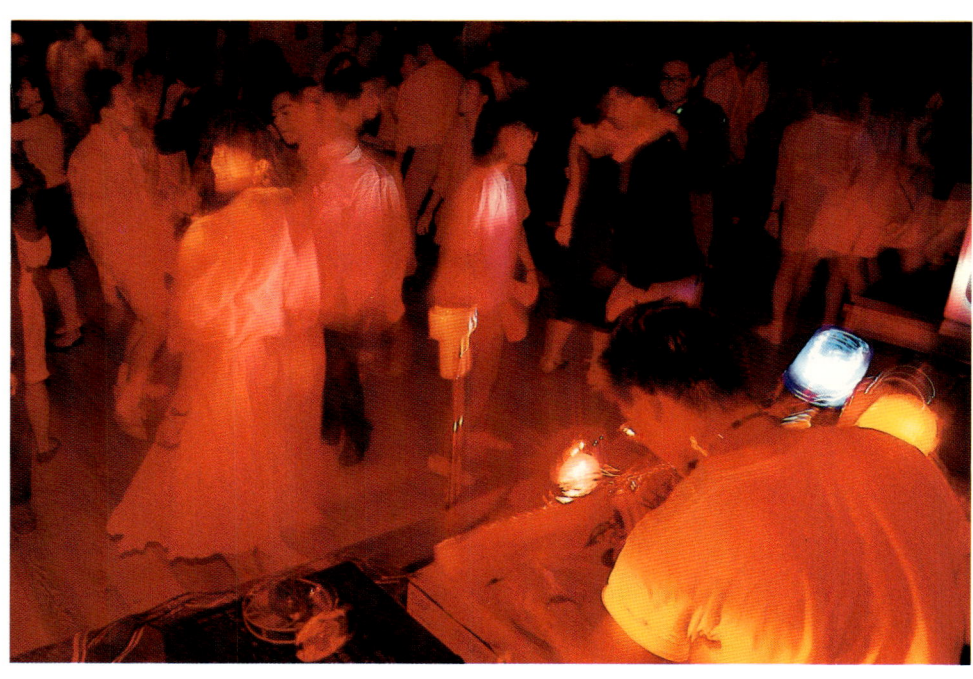

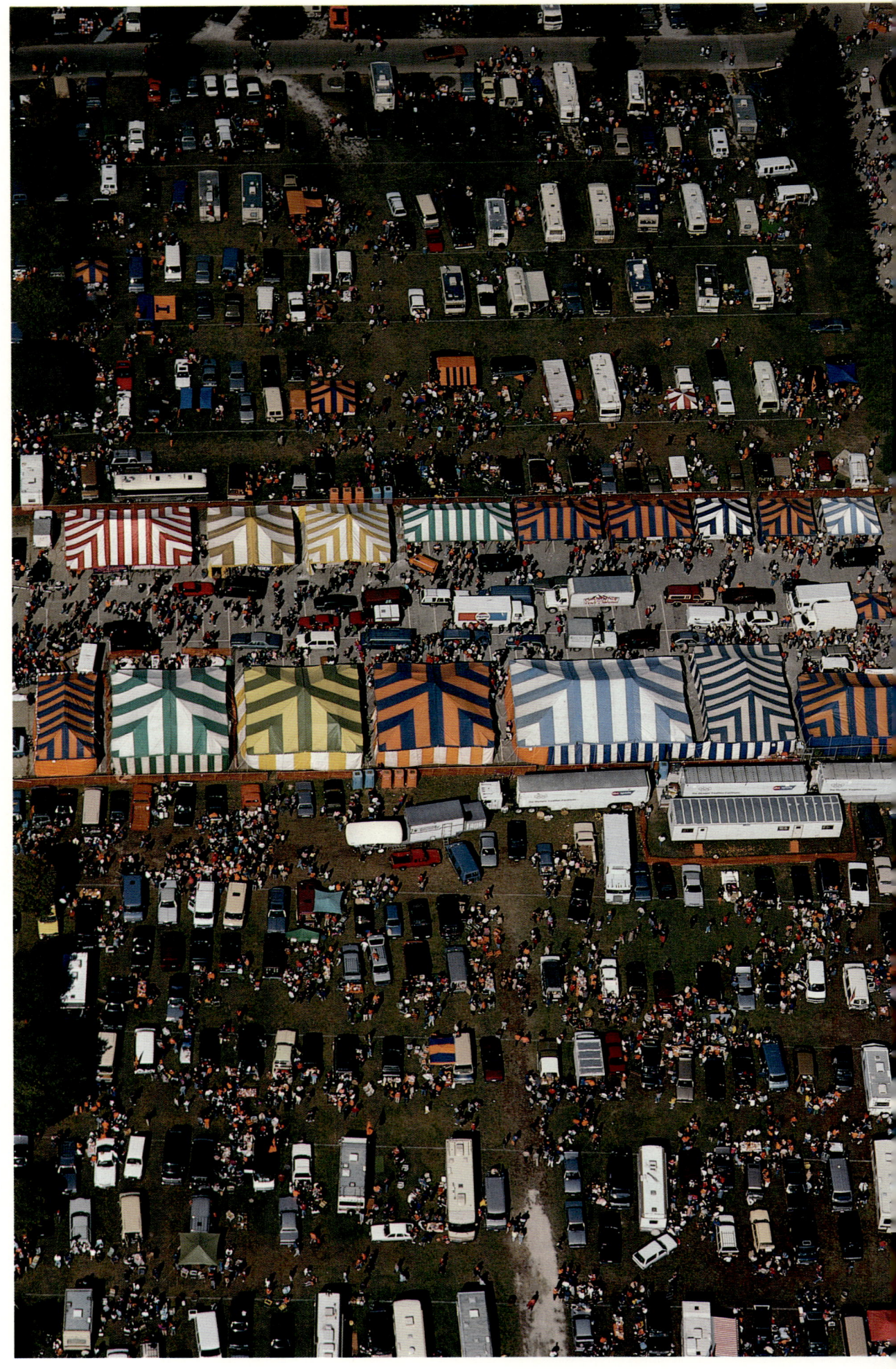

55

Homecoming

The Memorial Stadium is the largest and most imposing structure on the campus. The building has had a far-reaching influence on the University. Aside from the very useful purpose it serves and the inspiring architectural impression it makes in the campus ensemble, its greatest value is due to the fact that it is a memorial, built with funds subscribed by alumni and friends, and by virtue of this ideal has focused the attention of the people of the state ... It has served to give them a common interest in the institution, and as a result has created a very great bond between the University and the outside world.

Leon Tilton and Thomas O'Donnell, *History of the Campus Plan*, 1930

61

Illini teams have won championships in all of the other sports, but it is usually football and basketball which attract the most fan interest among the college crowd. Many people now attending the University of Illinois will look back on their college days and refer to them as the "Butkus years" or the "Grabowski era." Old-timers who have seen them all still insist that the greatest football team Illinois has ever produced was a one-man gang named Harold "Red" Grange.

Bill Anderson in the *Daily Illini*, February, 1967

Assembly Hall

A hundred years of history at the University of Illinois have left a tangible record in the stones and bricks and steel and concrete of its three campuses. Obviously, without its physical plant a university could not exist, but buildings reflect many things other than pure utility. A campus is a diary of the times, reflecting the vigor of the University, the economic and social climate of the country and the changing tastes and ideas of each era.

Charles S. Havens in preface to *100 years of Campus Architecture* by Allen Weller, 1968

Altgeld Hall

Altgeld Hall's handsome Romanesque tower, rough surfaces of a hard, pink sandstone, excellent detail and asymmetrical but balanced composition, make it a notable period piece. The only building of Romanesque design on campus, Altgeld Hall reflects with a considerable distinction the style which, in this country, is chiefly associated with architect H.H. Richardson.

Allen Weller in *100 Years of Campus Architecture*, 1968

English Building

To those on either coast it may seem an anomaly that the world's leading supercomputer mecca rises out of the cornfields of central Illinois. But transforming the University of Illinois campus into the Supercomputer Capital of the World was not such a great leap for the high-technology gurus who have kept the University's engineering school on technology's cutting edge for years.

Chicago Tribune, September, 1986

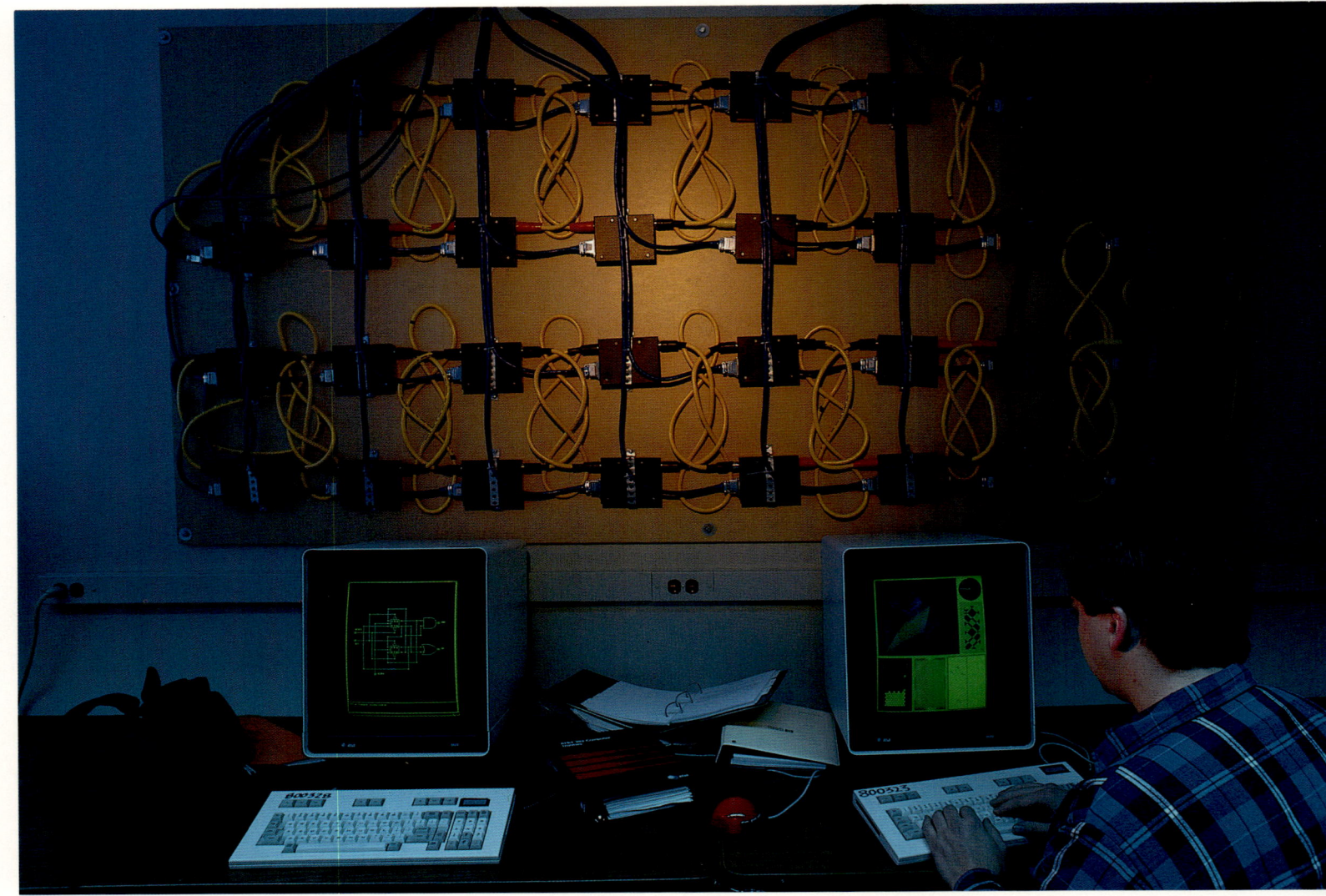

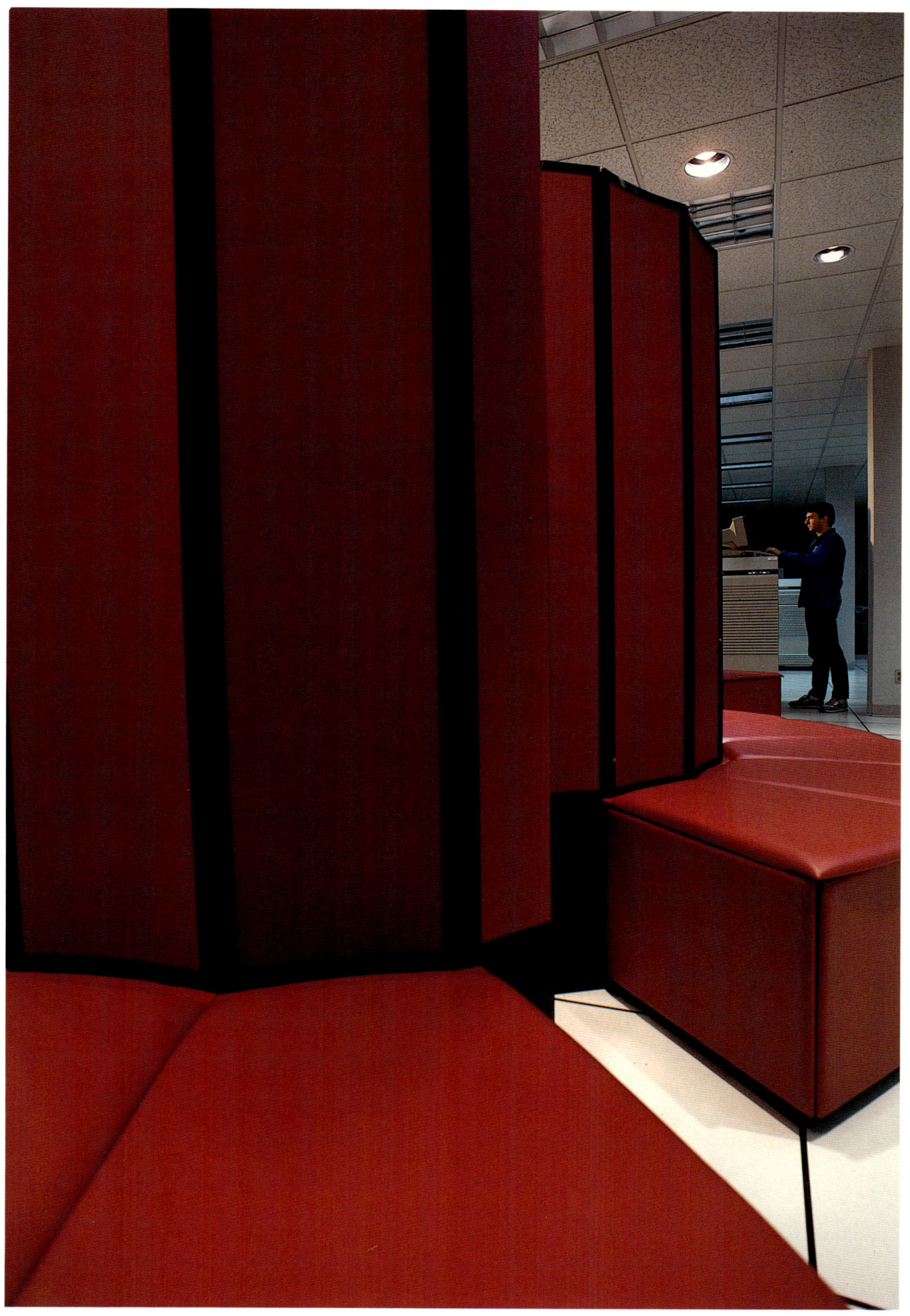

Cray Supercomputer

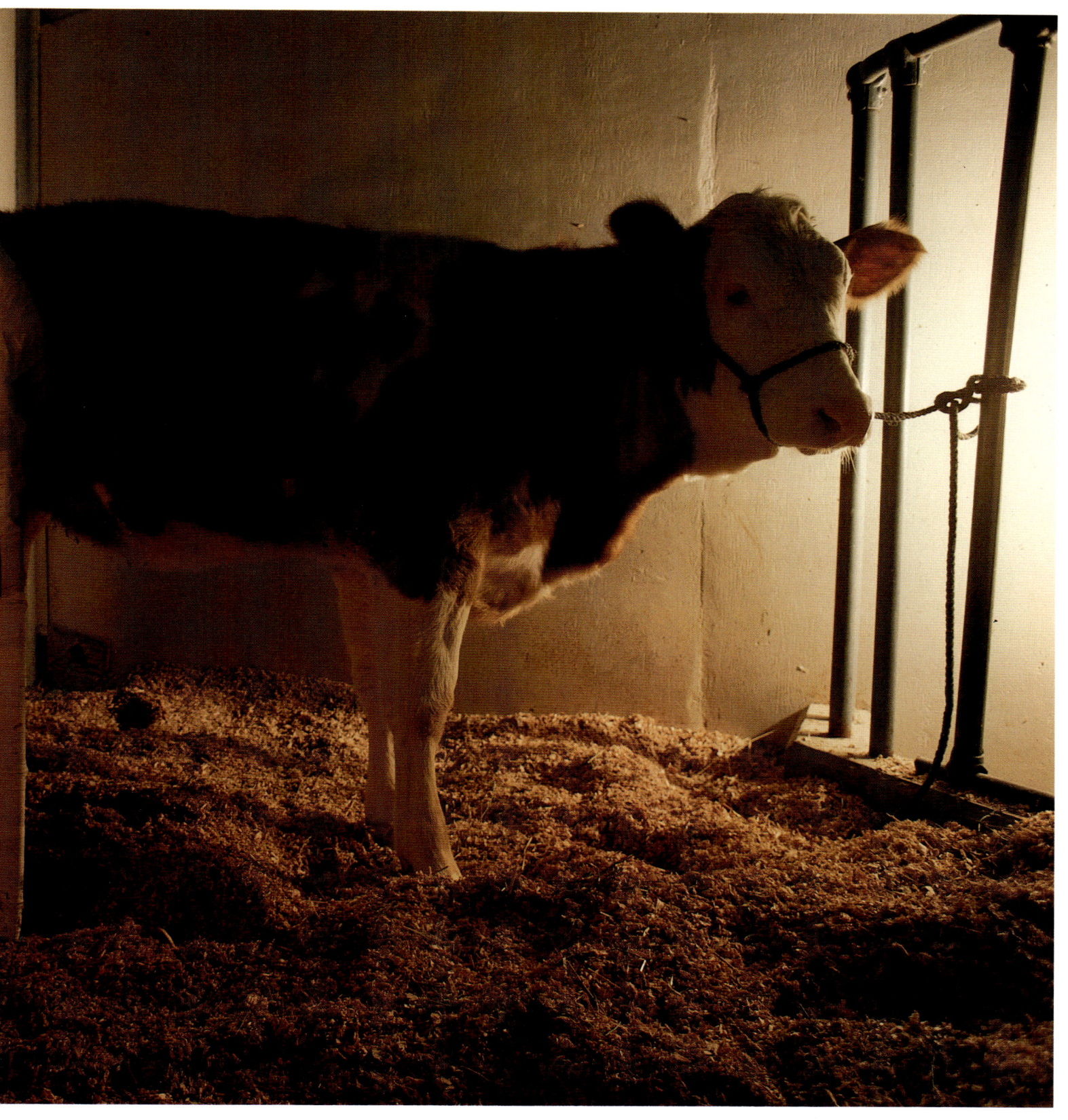

Stock Pavilion

Rodin's "Adam," Allerton Park

The Quad

It is difficult to think of a finer example of a modern adaptation of Georgian style than the Illini Union with its stately portico, four pairs of columns, well-conceived pediment, and octagonal cupola with clock and interesting skyline. The interior was designed and executed with particular care and elegance and has remained in impeccable condition.

Allen Weller, *100 Years of Campus Architecture*, 1968

Wesley Spire

Foellinger Great Hall, Krannert Center

This is a memorable day for me. Coming as it does from a great University that stands for some of the finest traditions of higher education, this honorary degree has a meaning for me beyond the flattering citation. So I am grateful to be honored by this renowned University. I have watched it grow in significance and size for fifty years, and like all sons of Illinois, my pride in it has grown with it.

Adlai Stevenson, Honors Day Convocation, 1964

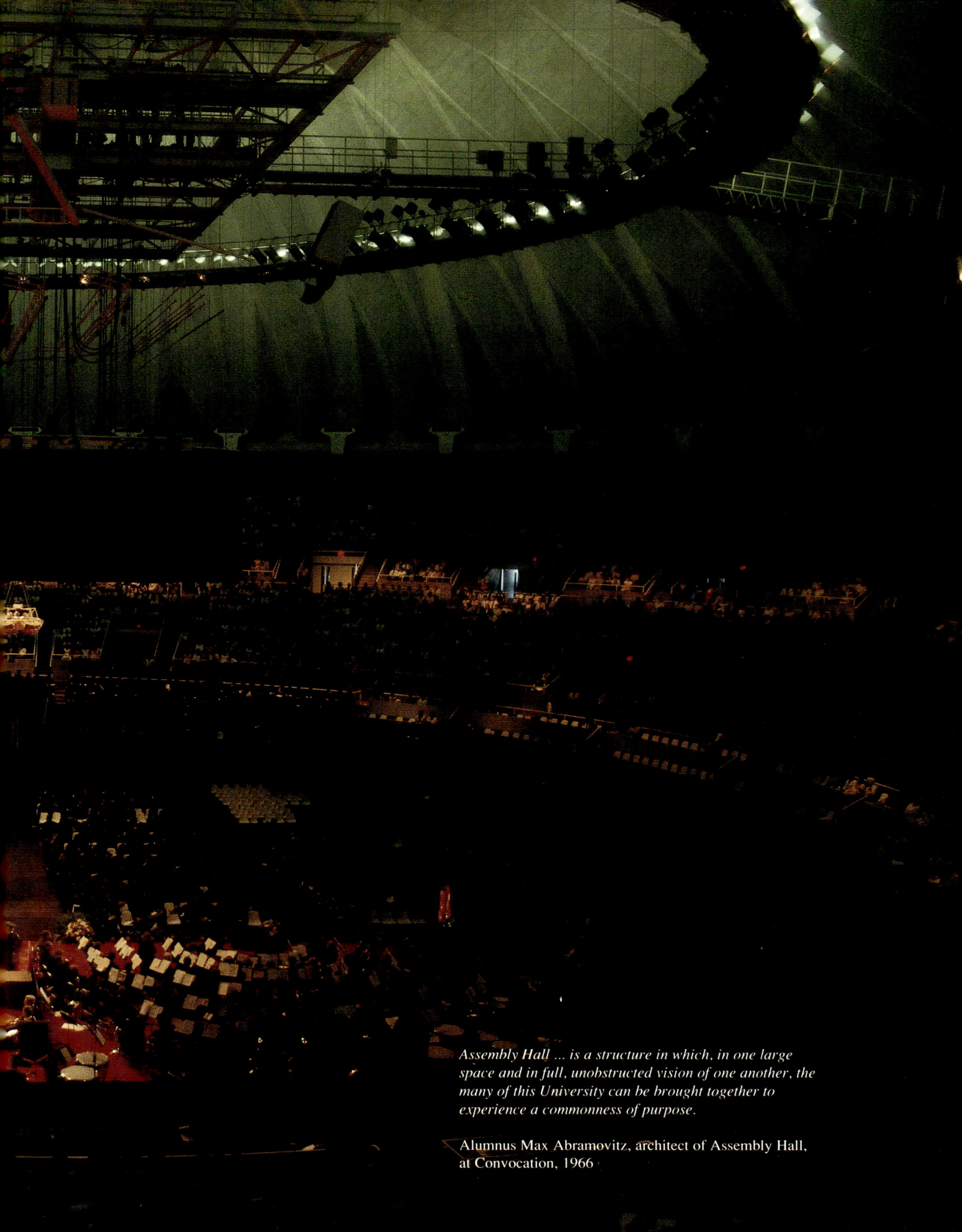

Assembly Hall ... is a structure in which, in one large space and in full, unobstructed vision of one another, the many of this University can be brought together to experience a commonness of purpose.

Alumnus Max Abramovitz, architect of Assembly Hall, at Convocation, 1966

92

We have an ambition to send forth to the great industries of the world, not people who are puffed up by some little smatterings of science, but clear-headed scholars, people of fully developed minds — fit leaders of those great productive arts by which the world's civilization is fed and furnished.

Dr. John Milton Gregory, Inaugural ceremonies March 11, 1868

LOOKING BACK AT

THE UNIVERSITY OF ILLINOIS

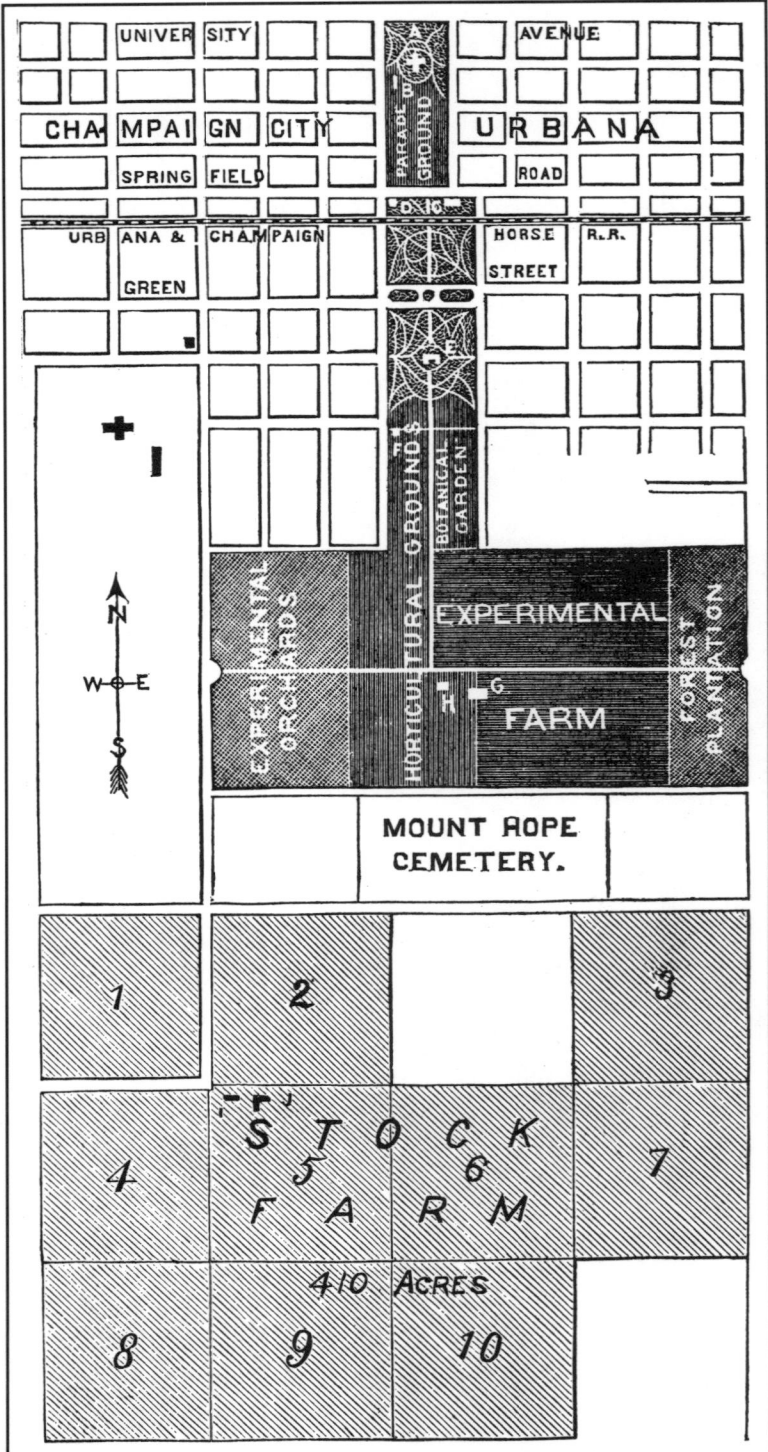

This map of 1871 shows the land holdings of the new University and divisions recommended by the Horticulture Committee.

The University's first building was used by the more than 100 students for almost every school activity: as a classroom, dormitory (the top two floors), chapel and clubhouse. The building was known by the students as "the Elephant." It stood alone on an often-muddy plain surrounded by cow pastures.

The Drill Hall and Machine Shop was the University's second building, erected in 1872.

This 1874 view of the campus is from a window in University Hall, and shows the main building, the Boneyard, the Drill Hall and Green Street.

Baseball was the game at the University in the 1870's. Here a group of students plays on a makeshift field near the main building.

A severe wind storm collapsed a section of wall from the main building in 1880.

In 1888, students typically gathered in "Boarding House Clubs," one of which is pictured above.

Sixteen men and a captain made up a military company in the late 1880's. Military training was a standard part of a young man's college education. At left, a company lines up for a photo in front of the Drill Hall.

A milestone in 1897: caps and gowns are first worn at the Illinois commencement ceremony.

Philomathean Literary Society Hall in 1888.

Alethenai Hall was the assembly place for the women's literary society.

This scene was typical of classes held in the lecture room in the early days of the College of Medicine, Chicago.

In 1911, President William H. Taft visited the University to review the University Battalion at the request of his good friend, President Edmund Janes James.

"Homecoming" began as a collegiate activity at the University of Illinois in 1910. This photograph, taken during the famous game, lets us know that Illinois beat the University of Chicago by a field goal, 3-0.

A campanile was a suggestion arising from the Campus Plan of 1913. This sketch of a clock tower was prepared by Professor James M. White, who had been appointed Supervising Architect by President Edmund Janes James in 1910. It was never erected.

Memorial Stadium was the largest and most imposing structure on the campus when it was built in 1924. Its cost in those days was considerable — $2 million — but its seating capacity was 70,000, and all the seats were needed to witness the heroics of the Illinois star of this era, Harold "Red" Grange. Illinois, with Grange scoring four long touchdowns in the first 12 minutes, beat Michigan 39-14 in the dedication game.

The Smith Memorial Music Hall, as it was called when it was built, was the home of the School of Music for many years. Now Smith Hall, its performance hall and practice rooms are still used today by many music students.

The front of the Woman's Building, circa 1917. This building was designed and built by the prestigious firm of McKim, Mead and White, and was considered by many to be the jewel of all campus architecture for many years. It is now known as the English Building.

The Armory is shown here in 1927, after a formal entrance, corridors and surrounding rooms were added to the central drill hall.

The Agriculture Building, now Davenport Hall, was part of the great expansion era of the University in the early 1900's. It was the first large building positioned south of University Hall.

The three portals of the Library are typical of the formal Georgian style the University chose for the south campus buildings in the 1920's. This view was taken around 1930.

This photo from 1917 shows, left to right, Harker Hall, University Hall, and the Library (later known as Altgeld Hall).

The capacity crowd at the stadium dedication game, 1924.

Illinois' famous 1943 basketball team, the "Whiz Kids."

Illinois' most famous baseball player, Lou Boudreau, who went on to star for many years in the major leagues.

The immortal Harold "Red" Grange, circa 1924.

Red Sox player and Illinois alumnus Jake Stahl bats against his old team.

In what sportscasters hailed as "the Comeback of the Year," Pete Elliott, right, coached the Illini to a 17-7 victory over the University of Washington in the 1964 Rose Bowl.

A favorite gathering spot for students was Hanley's in the Bradley Arcade on South Wright Street. Honking your horn out front got curb service.

The Auditorium, one of the University's most enduring landmarks, is shown here in 1918. The rededicated Foellinger Auditorium today is a multipurpose facility, used for lectures, classrooms and concerts.

A familiar scene to many Illinois alums — the Broadwalk in a beautiful winter snow. That's the English Building, formerly Bevier Hall, in the background.

The post-war professional colleges of medicine, dentistry and pharmacy were located here on the University of Illinois - Chicago campus.

This was the Lily Pond on South Campus in 1952. Now gone, it was on a site near Allen Hall and Illini Grove. It was a popular place for walks and conversation. That's the Women's Gym in the background.